WORLD'S ★ GREATEST

SPORTS BRAWLS

JOHN McGRAN

LONGSTREET
Atlanta, Georgia

Published by
Longstreet Press, Inc.
A subsidiary of Cox Newspapers,
A subsidiary of Cox Enterprises, Inc.
2140 Newmarket Parkway
Suite 122
Marietta, GA 30067

Printed in the United States of America
1st printing, 1998
World's Greatest Sports Brawls is produced by becker&mayer!, Kirkland, Washington.
Library of Congress Catalog Card Number: 97-76256
ISBN: 1-56352-476-7

Electronic film prep by Overflow Graphics Incorporated, Forest Park, GA

Special thanks to Tim Harrod

Jacket photograph: Linda Kaye/AP

Book and jacket design by Burtch Bennett Hunter

To my wonderful wife Barbara and our beautiful baby boy Jonathan. You've proved to this dreamer that fairy tales can indeed come true. And to my mother Catherine, who once upon a time gave me a great beginning for my life story.

CONTENTS

FOREWORD

Welcome to the wild world of sports. It's a savage place where chaos is king and brawl men are created equal — at least until the first punch is thrown. While historians cannot pinpoint the exact time and date of the first-ever sports brawl, it would come as no great surprise if one day scientists stumble upon a cave drawing that depicts a pair of prehistoric men knockin' the hell out of each other over possession of a dinosaur dropping that's been molded into a shape strikingly similar to a modern-day football.

Sadly, there seems to be no limit to the atrocities attributed to athletes — whether they be men or women. Such shameful savagery is by no means confined to the rough and tough contact sports such as football, hockey, soccer or rugby. Brawling knows no boundaries. This collection includes outrageous acts of unsportsmanlike conduct committed by golfers, jockeys, bicyclists . . . even water polo players!

Due to the sheer number of games played, baseball appears to be the all-around best sport for tales of bad behavior by tantrum-throwing athletes. The pro players may be mega-millionaires, but many spoiled sports stars come up plenty short in the sense department.

Hockey, of course, has had more than its share of shameful moments. Other than boxing or ultimate fighting, no other sport allows its athletes such freedom to dish out fierce beatings in exchange for a few minutes spent resting in the penalty box. Outside the arena, such teeth-rattling fisticuffs would bring felony charges and prison sentences. But when the same crime is committed on ice, the perpetrator is sometimes penalized — and frequently praised by fans as a hard-hitting enforcer!

The sports pages are peppered with stories of poor sports who won't hesitate to attempt out-punching opponents who are outplaying them. There's a growing danger to these despicable displays of bad sportsmanship. Whether they like it or not, top athletes are role models for many young, impressionable athletes. When a competitive kid sees his sports hero sucker-punching an opponent — or worse yet, an official — he may think it's acceptable behavior.

Submitted for your disapproval:

- Officials in Southern California reacted to an outbreak of brawls among high school basketball players by banning the traditional postgame goodwill handshakes in 1994.

- Several basketball players and their coach attacked referees with punches, kicks and a metal chair when the officials called an early stop to a 1996 game in Kenton County, Kentucky. The refs felt the on-court action between the teams of 12- to 14-year-olds had gotten out of hand.

Former heavyweight boxer Ron Lyle once said: "America wasn't built on going to church; it was built on violence. I express America in the ring." Laurel German, a lecturer with the Chico State sociology department, agrees with the fighter's philosophy. "It's innate biologically; we have built-in aggression and it's also part of our cultural pattern that's taught. We call it nature versus nurture. It's like which came first: the chicken or the egg. Both exist and both are necessary."

— J. M.

WORLD'S ★ GREATEST

SPORTS BRAWLS

NOLAN RYAN DELIVERS NOOGIE PUNCHES TO THE NOGGIN OF ROBIN VENTURA.

Chapter 1

TAKE ME OUT TO THE BRAWL GAME . . .

BATTERED UP!

On a hot August night in 1993, hard-throwing Hall of Famer Nolan Ryan easily struck out . . . make that out struck Chicago White Sox third baseman Robin Ventura, who, after a beaning, had foolishly charged the legendary Texas Rangers pitcher. To the fans, the one-sided mugging on the mound more closely resembled a professional wrestling match than a classic baseball brouhaha. In a slapstick that could have come straight out of a silly "Three Stooges" short, villain Ventura landed on the receiving end of rapid-fire head punches pitched by the King of the K — which in this case stood for knuckle sandwiches rather than strikeouts. Sporting the nimble moves of a master matador, 46-year-old Ryan sidestepped his incensed assailant and then corralled the bull-headed batter with a slick headlock. The Texas tornado then embarrassed red-faced Robin, using his fists instead of fastballs to poke away at the punchless player. Before players and umps broke up the brawl, Ryan delivered a hailstorm of hits to the head of his defenseless foe. Perhaps some day Ventura will put a positive spin on his shameful run-in with Ryan. The first-rate player who proved to be a third-rate fighter could brag to his grandkids about the day he got multiple hits off baseball's all-time strikeout artist (5,714 total Ks), the fireballing phenom who tossed a spectacular seven no-hitters during an awesome 27-year career.

A WHACK ON THE WILD SIDE

For Hall of Fame pitcher Juan Marichal of the San Francisco Giants it was One! Two! Three! strikes and out of the game after the hot-headed hurler used his baseball bat to batter the

UPI/Corbis-Bettmann

PITCHER JUAN MARICHAL SWINGS A MEAN BAT . . .
TOWARD THE HEAD OF OPPOSING CATCHER JOHN ROSEBORO.

brains of Los Angeles Dodgers catcher John Roseboro on August 22, 1965. Madman Marichal was Juan unhappy camper after Roseboro flung the ball a bit too close to the batter's ear. The peeved pitcher showed his displeasure by taking three killer cuts at the catcher's cranium. The Candlestick Park crowd went wild over Marichal's startling third-inning assault. The savage triple play of pops quickly triggered a full-scale donnybrook on the diamond. Poor Roseboro had no chance to fight back as Juan wildly whacked away at his helmeted head. Luckily, his Dodger teammates swarmed the field and dis-armed the brawling Batman before he could connect for a few more horrifying hits. The savage attack left a nasty notch in Roseboro's noggin and delayed the game for 14 min-utes. Play resumed once officials were assured that the bat-wielding brawler had been escorted to the showers. Over his 16-year career, Marichal rang up sterling stats such as a 243-142 won-loss record and a 2.89 earned run average. But while it was pitching prowess that earned the Dominican dominator a ticket to Canton, Ohio, it was the hurler's hitting that left a mark on the game — and a scar on Roseboro's skull.

BELLE OF THE BRAWL

A May 31, 1996, brouhaha between the Cleveland Indians and Milwaukee Brewers led to the fifth suspension in six seasons for one of Major League Baseball's all-time bad boys, Albert Belle. Cleveland's short-fused outfielder was booted for five games, fined $25,000 and ordered to undergo temper-control counseling after he brutally bowled over Brewers second baseman Fernando Vina in an attempt to bust up a double play. The fierce forearm Belle delivered to the infielder's face lit the fuse for the ten-minute free-for-all that followed in the ninth. An earlier collision between Belle and Vina occurred in the third inning of the game at Milwaukee. Despite a bump from baserunner Belle, Vina tagged him for one out, then threw to first to complete a double play. But after Belle was hit by a pitch and took first base in the eighth, he made sure history wouldn't repeat itself — by plowing Vina into the ground and

AP photo/Peter Zuzga

BELLE MAY BE OUT, BUT FERNANDO VINA IS DOWN.

breaking up the double play chance. All hell then broke loose when Cleveland pitcher Julian Tavarez fired a fastball behind Brewers batter Mike Matheny to make up for Belle's beaning. Matheny was miffed enough to charge the mound — a move that emptied both benches. When it was all over, Tavarez, who knocked an umpire to the ground, and Matheny, who

AP photo/Tom Pidgeon

ALBERT BELLE REGULARLY LOSES HIS HEAD . . .
AND SOMETIMES HIS HELMET.

attacked the opposing pitcher, were each tagged with five-day suspensions.

By the time he was traded to the Chicago White Sox in 1997, Belle's blow-ups had taken their toll on his team, on the league and on his bank account. Perhaps his worst behavior was displayed at the 1996 World Series. That's when the outrageous Indian went on the warpath and verbally assaulted NBC reporter Hannah Storm with a curse-filled tirade that was aired on national television. Belle was blasted by baseball officials who handed him a league record $50,000 fine. That very same month Belle rang up a $100 fine for hopping into a pickup truck and racing after teens who tossed eggs at his house on Halloween. An Ohio court found Belle guilty of reckless operation of a motor vehicle. Every year from 1991 to 1994 the 6'1", 190-pound superstar was suspended for offenses ranging from throwing a ball at a heckler to charging the mound to corking his bat. In April 1996, he intentionally beaned a *Sports Illustrated* photographer with a hard-thrown ball. Then a month later, Belle gave baseball yet another blemish by badmouthing a fan who wanted to exchange Albert's home-run ball for another valuable souvenir.

PROMOTION'S A BIG HIT

The intent was admirable, but the execution was oh, so deplorable when the home town Durham Bulls gave a black eye to a "Strike Out Domestic Violence" promotion by brawling with the visiting Winston-Salem Warthogs on May 22, 1995. The vicious clash between the Carolina League's Class A ballclubs resulted in one player being rushed to a hospital — unconscious and with fewer teeth than when he arrived at the ballpark — and a total of 10 players taking early showers. The savage third-inning free-for-all was triggered by a beanball delivered by Warthog pitcher Glen Cullop. The pitch earned Bulls batter John Knott a free trip to first base — and the 'Hog hurler an ambulance ride and a future date with his dentist. The Bulls may play minor league baseball, but at that moment they sure provided plenty of major league mayhem by stampeding out of the dugout and onto the diamond where teammate Knott had already charged the mound and was mixing it up with Cullop. The hot-headed hosts proceeded to welcome their Warthog guests with a medley of punches and knuckle sandwiches. So, what was planned as a noble anti-violence promotion came off as a despicable "do as we say, not as we do" demonstration. Rather than strike a blow against domestic violence, the basebrawlers chose instead to strike out at each other. Game officials weathered the hailstorm of haymakers, then went to work doling out the post-fight punishment. As the kayoed Warthog hurler was being carted off by medics, another 10 players were being herded to the showers. League officials also socked it to the penalized players, hitting them where it really hurt — their wallets. The bad boys of baseball were slapped with fines that added up to a record-setting $6,000 and suspensions that totaled a butt-numbing 124 games.

NO WAY TO TREAT A LADY

Ladies and gentlemen . . . were in short supply when possibly the first-ever mixed-sex sports melee erupted in 1997. The coed combatants: the Colorado Silver Bullets, a barn-

AP photo/Sonny Lofton

THE SILVER BULLETS PROVE THEY DON'T NEED ANY LONE RANGER.

storming baseball team made up entirely of women, and the Americus Travelers, a squad of 18-and-under males from Georgia. Forget everything you ever heard about women being the weaker sex. These belles of the brawl more than held their own, tagging the teen Travelers for fistfuls of hits — the kind that never appear in the box score. The ninth-inning fight was triggered by a beanball that bonked Kim Braatz-Voisard on the back. It was batter upset as the Silver Bullet centerfielder suddenly charged the mound — and the pitcher who had dared laugh out loud after intentionally tattooing his target. Kim didn't have to stalk alone. Her Coors comrades poured onto the field ready to exercise their women's rights — and lefts. When fans began spilling onto the field, one frustrated official threatened to call the cops. When the diamond clutter was cleared and brawl-starting Braatz-Voisard was ejected, the bad-mannered boys of summer fought their way back from a 6-0 deficit and went on to win the shameful slugfest 10-6. Silver Bullets general manager Phil Niekro, a genuine Hall of Fame hurler, threw his support behind his scrappy team. "As good a baseball brawl as I've ever seen," he proudly proclaimed. "Some of our players got in some pretty good licks. And some of our players got hit. I've seen it before in baseball, but never with women."

PITCHER, IF YOU WILL . . .

In 1995, a crazed Cubs fan made a major error in judgment when he leaped from his seat and raced across Wrigley Field to pick a fight with Chicago reliever Randy Myers, who had just served up an eighth inning homer during a key stretch-run ballgame. At 6'1" and 210 pounds, the imposing pitcher held much more than just an advantage in size. Myers was also a highly-trained martial arts expert! Cubs players rushed to the mound — more to save the on-field intruder from a major league beating than to protect their pitcher. Myers saw his attacker in plenty of time to effortlessly floor the beer-fueled fan with a simple takedown move. The cool-headed Cubs closer then kept the kook pinned to the turf until stadium security made their way to the mound. "Randy's the wrong guy to mess with," said Chicago third baseman Howard Johnson. "The fan is lucky he's still alive."

AP photo

MYERS GIVES A DEVOTED FAN MORE THAN AN AUTOGRAPH.

A GIANT MESS

Los Angeles Dodgers outfielder Reggie Smith got himself into a Giant mess when he went up into the stands at San Francisco's Candlestick Park to brawl with foul-mouthed fans on September 25, 1981. For five innings, Smith put up with the steady stream of put-downs from the jeering Giants fans seated behind the Dodgers' dugout. But he snapped in the sixth, shocking his coaches and teammates — and the Candlestick crowd — by bolting from the safety of the Dodger bench and scampering into the hostile home crowd to tangle with one of the biggest-mouthed bleacher bums. Reggie managed to get his mitts on the stunned heckler, but by doing so he had placed himself in the midst of what

AP photo

REGGIE SMITH DECIDES HE'S HAD ENOUGH FAN ABUSE . . .

had quickly become a bloodthirsty mob. Smith picked up a couple of hard hits before he was rescued by his teammates and returned to the field. Alas, Smith's return was short-lived. Game officials immediately suspended the L.A. outfielder. Meanwhile, stadium security escorted eight unruly individuals away for questioning.

The near-riot wasn't the first time Smith got into a fracas with a fan. On June 8, 1977, the 17-year veteran ballplayer had to be wrestled to the ground at Wrigley Field by Dodger teammate Dusty Baker to prevent him from ringing the neck of a vocal Chicago Cubs fan. The first-inning fiasco fizzled as fast as it began thanks to Baker's bear hug. Smith later said he objected to the dirty names pitched his way by the foul-mouthed fan.

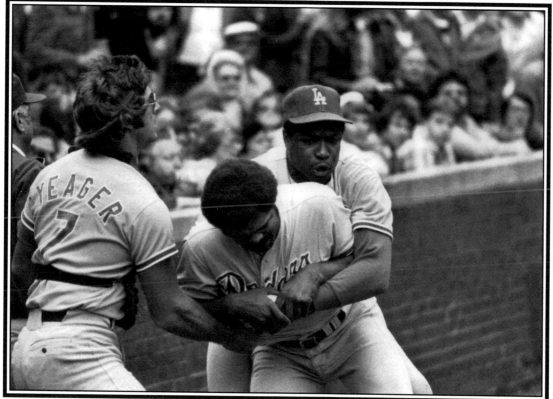

UPI/Corbis-Bettmann

TEAMMATE DUSTY BAKER HAS HAD ENOUGH OF REGGIE SMITH.

SOMETIMES A GESTURE
SAYS IT ALL . . .

CARDINAL SIN

St. Louis slugger Garry Templeton didn't like the chorus of boos he heard from the home crowd after he struck out in the first inning of an August 26, 1981, game against the San Francisco Giants. So the short-tempered shortstop stunned the Ladies Day crowd at Busch

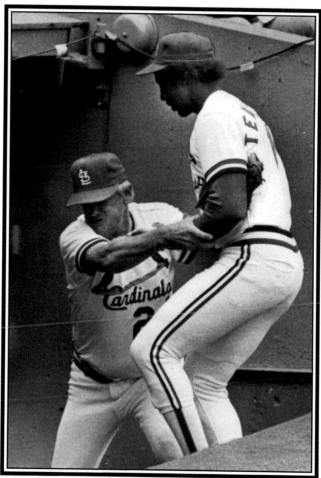

UPI/Corbis-Bettmann

AND WHITEY HERZOG
HAS SEEN ENOUGH!

13

Stadium by flashing an obscene gesture. Similar jeers and gestures were exchanged for another two innings. By that time, home plate ump Bruce Froemming had seen enough of Templeton's talents and responded with a hand signal of his own — the thumb jerk that meant some jerk was being ejected. But before he headed for the showers, Templeton treated the fans to a few more memorable maneuvers, including a defiant crotch grab. The next grab was made by incensed St. Louis manager Whitey Herzog, who locked on to Templeton's arm and yanked him down the cement steps leading into the Cardinals' dugout. There the shameless shortstop and the cardinal-red coach nearly came to blows. It took a flock of Cardinals to quell the commotion. Herzog later fined Templeton $5,000, ordered him to make a public apology and benched the bad-mannered ballplayer indefinitely.

ROSE 'N' BOOM!

A bench-clearing brawl bloomed during Game 3 of the 1973 National League Championship Series after Cincinnati Reds baserunner Pete Rose bowled over New York Mets infielder Bud Harrelson. Charlie Hustle may have planted Harrelson deep in the Shea Stadium dirt, but not before the Mets second baseman completed a nifty double play throw to first to end the fifth inning. The area around second base instantly became a wrestling mat with Rose and Harrelson the featured fighters. The tussling twosome were knotted up and flailing furiously to and fro as their teammates stormed onto the field for some fisticuffs of their own. Rose's steamrolling of the second sacker failed to spark the sputtering Reds. Cincinnati dropped the game 9-2 . . . and then the series, 3-2, to New York.

AP/Wide World

CAN YOU FIND PETE ROSE IN THIS MÉNAGE À TROIS?

SHORT STOPS

• During a 1970 game, Kansas Royals batter Lou Pinella charged the mound after being hit by a pitch from Jim Perry of the Minnesota Twins. "I shouldn't have picked on a guy who had a brother pitching in the big leagues," Pinella recalled. "From that day on, every time Jim Perry saw me, he knocked me down. And every time Gaylord Perry saw me, he knocked me down, too."

• At the start of a Northern League minor league baseball game in 1956, Winnipeg pitcher Carlos Thome was tossing his warm-up pitches when St. Cloud lead-off hitter Nick Tedesco started inching toward home plate. Thome responded by brushing back the batter with a fastball. Tedesco retaliated by flinging his bat at the mound. A bench-clearing brawl broke out. By the time the game began, both Thome and Tedesco were missing from the lineups — both players had been suspended.

• Meg Porter never dreamed she'd become a beanball victim, but that's what happened to the schoolteacher from Batavia, Ohio, when she attended a Cincinnati Reds baseball game in 1991. From her center-field seat, Porter watched the home team down the Pittsburgh Pirates. But despite picking up a save in relief, Reds pitcher Rob Dibble was upset with his performance. He vented his anger after the win by turning to the outfield and hurling the baseball toward the center-field stands nearly 400 feet away. Of course, the ball beaned poor Porter on the elbow. She was fitted with a cast and missed several days of work. Dibble was fined by his team.

• Moments after St. Louis Browns hurler Earl Harrist plunked two Boston Red Sox batters in a 1952 game at Fenway Park, a one-legged Red Sox fan hobbled onto the field on crutches, made his way to the mound and scolded the red-faced pitcher — much to the home crowd's delight. The aggravated fan thought Harrist had taken the city of Boston's nickname — Bean Town — too literally.

• Cincinnati Reds first baseman Babe Young flew into such a blind rage during a 1948 game that he forgot about baseball — and instead turned into a wrestler. After knocking a double off the left-field wall, Young complained that Pittsburgh Pirates shortstop Stan Rojek had intentionally interfered with his baserunning. Without calling for time, Babe bolted from second base and hopped on the back of Rojek, triggering a wild free-for-all. Pittsburgh pitcher Vic Lombardi picked up the ball, which was still in play, reached through the pile of players — and tagged out the Young and the reckless.

THE RANGERS GET AN EARLY SHOWER.

Chapter 2

THREE JEERS FOR THE FANS!

BEER BASH FALLS FLAT

Cleveland Indians fans began foaming at the mouth with anger once officials ordered the taps turned off during ill-fated Nickel Beer Night on June 4, 1974. The game was supposed to pit the Indians against the Texas Rangers, but it ended up with the visitors fearing for their lives as they fought hand-to-hand with the beer-muscled masses who poured out of the stands in the ninth inning. The drunken horde numbered in the hundreds and had its collective blurry eye on Texas outfielder Jeff Burroughs. The Rangers rushed to the defense of their outnumbered teammate, exchanged punches with some of the inebriated invaders, then beat a hasty retreat to the dugout where manager Billy Martin — a man never known to back down from a fight — armed himself with a bat to fend off the fans who dared come close to his players. The game was never completed. The Rangers were awarded a forfeit win — but not before the fired-up fans kept the team pinned down in its dugout with a fierce barrage of fireworks. The terrifying riot left one umpire and four Texas players injured — and put a cork in any future bargain beer promotions in Cleveland.

BUT THE SIGN SAYS TO RETURN TO YOUR SEATS . . .

BLAME THAT TUNE

Chicago White Sox officials were more concerned with stayin' alive than playin' baseball when they unceremoniously canceled the second game of a scheduled doubleheader with Detroit on July 12, 1979. There was no dancing around the reason for the sudden postponement. The weather wasn't to blame. It was a flood of beer-fueled fans who stormed from their bleacher seats and onto the Comisky Park ballfield to roar their approval of a raucous and rolling Anti-Disco promotional stunt that proved to have plenty more Sox appeal than organizers anticipated. The disco beat took a battering that night. The first blow was struck by a local disc jockey who fired up the fans by detonating an explosive buried deep beneath thousands of disco records piled in centerfield. But the final blow was struck by the spectators who refused to leave the playing field despite repeated requests. Disco music had been officially laid to rest, but the Sox fans insisted on one long and joyfully loud last dance on its grave.

DODGER BALL

Meanwhile, San Francisco was the scene of another violent brawl for the visiting Dodgers in 1986. And this time Reggie Smith couldn't be blamed for the brouhaha — he had already retired. It was clearly frustrated San Fran fans who transformed Candlestick Park into a war zone after Los Angeles swept both ends of a doubleheader. The crowd flung golf balls and baseball bats at the victors. The Dodgers managed to dodge the projectiles and slip away unscathed, but San Fran team president Al Rosen was outraged and embarrassed by the bombardment. Comparing the Candlestick bleachers to a fierce World War II battle site, he proclaimed: "The beach at Okinawa was safer."

THE WILD BUNCH

The brawling really snowballed during a 1907 early-season baseball game between the New York Giants and Philadelphia Phillies. The snow-covered seats provided plenty of ammunition for those bundled-up fans who had braved the frigid weather conditions that were more suited to skiing. When the players tried to take the frozen field, they were greeted with a hailstorm of hard-packed snowballs heaved from the stands. The cold-boulder treatment made home plate umpire Bill Klem hot under the collar. The official ordered the besieged ballplayers to retreat — first to the dugouts and then to the locker rooms — when he proclaimed the game a forfeit win for the visiting Phillies.

> "I KNOW WHY THEY THREW IT AT ME.
> WHAT I CAN'T FIGURE OUT IS WHY
> THEY BROUGHT IT TO THE BALLPARK
> IN THE FIRST PLACE."
>
> — *St. Louis Cardinals outfielder Joe Medwick, after a barrage of fruit, garbage and cardboard boxes from Detroit fans in the left-field stands forced him to leave the seventh game of the 1934 World Series*

BIG MACK ATTACK

More than 30,000 fans celebrated the Philadelphia Phillies' final game at Connie Mack Stadium — a 2-1, 10-inning win over the Montreal Expos — by pillaging the place on October 1, 1970. The crazed crowd could barely restrain its mob mentality . . . or be

Temple University

"WHAT AM I BID FOR THIS FINE — SLIGHTLY USED — ROW OF SEATS?"

restrained by riot police who watched helplessly as the Phillies fanatics overran the 61-year-old ballpark. Nothing was safe from the savage souvenir hunters. Not the bleacher seats. Not the turf or infield dirt. Not even the bathroom fixtures. The guests at this infamous Woodchopper's Brawl ruined the dignified stadium-closing ceremony planned by the Philadelphia front office. They began to unbolt, unscrew or simply tear up anything they could get their hands on — in the seventh inning! About the only thing the riot police could salvage was home plate. Feeling like Custer's troops at Little Big Horn, the tough but out-manned cops cordoned off the small patch of playing field and bravely stood their ground as the unauthorized wrecking crew ran wild around them. "It was unreal," said Phillies pitcher Chris Short. "They were throwing seat slats at the guys in the bullpen and in the outfield the whole game. They were still pelting us even when some cops moved out by the fence."

MY CUP RUNNETH OVER

In 1990, University of Wisconsin officials quickly stepped in to stop what had become a home game tradition — students pelting each other with heavy plastic cups. One Badgers band member sustained a broken nose when she was whacked in the face with a cup stuffed with wet newspaper for weight. Such carnage was cut dramatically when the dangerous drinking cups were banned — and replaced with extra-lightweight containers. "Students are still throwing things," reported assistant athletic director Joel Maturi. "But nobody's getting hurt."

THIS PICTURE RATED R — FOR VIOLENCE.

AP photo

Chapter 3

DISORDER ON THE COURT

ONE-HIT BLUNDER

On December 9, 1977, Houston Rocket Rudy Tomjanovich was blasted into orbit by a savage sucker punch from Los Angeles Laker Kermit Washington. Rudy T never saw the roundhouse right that ripped into his face, fracturing his jaw, eye and cheek — and giving him a concussion for good measure. The 6'8" Houston forward was racing up court to break up a tussle between teammate Kevin Kunnert and Washington. But the moment Rudy reached the fight he was greeted fist-first by Special K. The 6'8", 230-pound slugger later claimed the "shot felt round the world" was delivered in defense as he caught sight of Tomjanovich coming up from behind. NBA Commissioner Larry O'Brien hit back by slamming Washington with a $10,000 fine and a 60-day suspension. The punishment hurt, but the pain was nothing compared to that suffered by Rudy T. He sat out the rest of the young season and underwent a grueling series of reconstructive surgeries to piece back together the peacekeeper's face.

SPIT-FOR-SPAT

Fiery Philadelphia 76ers forward Charles Barkley was spitting mad before he was bounced from a 1991 NBA game in New Jersey. Sir Charles was ejected and later fined $10,000 for spitting on an eight-year-old Nets fan who was seated several rows behind the Sixers bench. Barkley begged forgiveness from the little girl, whose enthusiasm had been disgustingly dampened by the superstar's awful outburst. The spitter later tried to explain that his salvo of saliva was meant for an obnoxious heckler seated in the vicinity of the victim. Whether or not bad aim was to blame, there would be no acquittal for Barkley's shameful spittle. League officials turned the expectorator into a spectator for Philly's next game and hit him with the five-figure fine. This was far from the first time Barkley's big mouth or his court gestures got him in big trouble. In 1985-86, the hack-happy player led the league in personal fouls, picking up 333 of 'em — and plenty of opposing players who got in his path. Barkley's off-court antics also attracted trouble in the form of barroom brawls and off-color comments. In 1992, after spending four hours in a Milwaukee jail following fisticuffs with a fan, he wisecracked: "I got superstar treatment. Everybody else got bologna and water. I got bologna and milk." In 1996, Charles twice ran afoul of the refs. After a loss to Seattle on February 13, the now-Phoenix forward was fined $5,000 for spiking the ball off the face of an official. Then on December 21 — after being traded to the Houston Rockets — Barkley was suspended for two games and fined $7,500 for bloodying the nose of an official with a finger poke.

Barkley may be the spittin' image of a player who embarrassed the NBA by spouting off on an innocent child. But seven-foot center Bill Cartwright once kayoed a kid seated at courtside for a 1991 home game in Chicago. The Bulls bully was often accused of using his extra-sharp elbows to clear opponents away from the basket. But boy did Cartwright bring a bonanza of bad vibes his way when he decked a nine-year-old fan while diving out of bounds for a loose ball. Bulls ball-boy-for-a-day Jim Fitzsimmons watched helplessly as the tower of terror toppled toward him — catching him just above his right eye with an elbow. But it was all's well that ends well. Jim forgave his favorite player after getting an ice pack and an autograph. "All I care about is I got to meet Bill Cartwright," boasted the blackened-eyed boy.

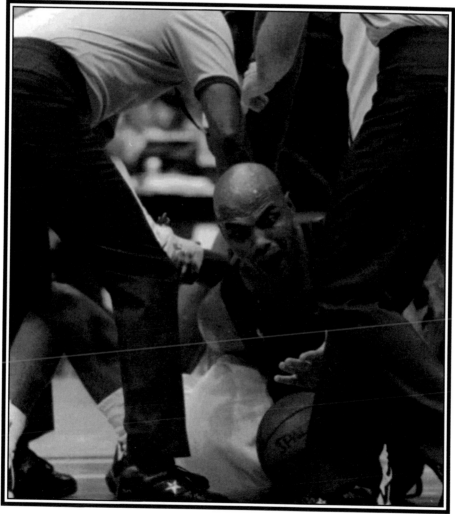

AP/Wide World

"HELP. I'VE FALLEN AND I CAN'T GET UP. PLUS I'M BLEEDING."

SCREAM 2 (POINTS)

Sometimes the playoff pressure just gets to you. When Barkley and San Antonio's Avery Johnson got tangled up (p.29) during the second Western Conference playoff game on April 28, 1996, Charles hit the ground and vented his rage in an audible scream. He quieted himself long enough for officials to call a jump ball on the play, and was discreet enough to keep relatively quiet throughout the game, even when the Suns lost to the Spurs by five points. A subsequent offer to endorse Shout Stain Remover™ fell through.

TURN UP THE HEAT

There was plenty of disorder on the court during Game 2 of the 1994 NBA playoff series featuring feuding Eastern Conference foes Atlanta Hawks and Miami Heat. A bench-clearing brawl broke out at the Atlanta Omni on April 30 shortly after Heat forward Grant Long locked horns with Hawks center Kevin Willis. Eventually, Atlanta police waded into the full-court fray in a desperate attempt to help the three-man officiating crew regain control. Ironically, the hardest hit was delivered by the livid Long who, in the heat of the moment, body-slammed Miami assistant coach Alvin Gentry, who had been attempting to hold back the 6'9", 245-pound power forward. Thanks to Long's short temper, the clobbered coach watched the rest of the game from a nearby hospital where he was treated for a fractured right hand. The Heat suffered a couple other bad breaks — Long was ejected from the game and Miami came out on the short end of a 104-86 final score.

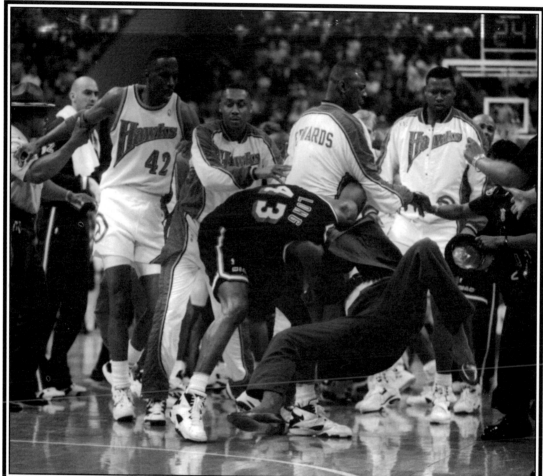

GRANT LONG FAILS TO NOTICE THE SUIT AND TIE.

AP/Wide World/John Bazemore

PILING ON . . . BASKETBALL STYLE.

SLAM DUNKED

There was even more Miami vice during Game 5 of the 1997 NBA Eastern Conference semifinals series as the Heat squared off with the New York Knicks. All hell broke loose following a free throw attempt. Miami forward P.J. Brown overheated when Knicks gnat Charlie Ward attempted to box-out the much bigger player by backing his butt into Brown's lower legs. In a flash, Brown blew his top, scooped up Ward like a sack of potatoes and body-slammed him behind the basket — smack in the middle of the off-court area crammed with photographers. With cameras flashing like disco strobe lights, a number of Knicks hustled off their nearby bench seats to bust a few moves on the bully Brown and his Heat buddies. Stern-faced NBA officials later slammed both squads for escalating the scrap. Hardest hit were the Knicks, who dared commit the cardinal sin of bolting from the bench to brawl. They lost five players including a trio of All-Stars — center Patrick Ewing, forward Charles Oakley and guard John Starks. The league did allow the Knicks, who held a commanding 3-1 lead in the best-of-seven series, to stagger the suspensions over Games 6 and 7. But New York's makeshift lineups couldn't hold on as Miami slipped by to face the Chicago Bulls in the Eastern Finals.

DENNIS THE MENACE

Dennis Rodman, without a doubt one of the most offensive defensive specialists to ever play in the NBA, was fined $25,000, ordered to undergo psychiatric counseling and suspended for 11 games after he lost his focus and kicked a courtside cameraman in the groin on January 15, 1997. Sadly, the despicable development during a game with the Minnesota Timberwolves was far from the first embarrassing brawl for the Chicago Bulls forward known almost as much for his kooky hair colors, bevy of body piercings and tattoo-covered skin,

REF TED BERNHARDT IS NOT HAVING FUN YET.

AP/Wide World/Bill Kostroun

AP/Wide World/Michael Conroy

ALONZO MOURNING GETS A FACE FULL OF RODMAN.

as he was for his run-ins with the refs, teammates and league officials. The 6'8" forward forged a high-paying career and collected a couple of championship rings with top-notch teams like Detroit, San Antonio and Chicago by concentrating on rebounding and defense. Unfortunately, Dennis' inability to control his outrageous on-court antics overshadowed his impressive athletic abilities. When he blatantly head-butted referee Ted Bernhardt in 1996, Rodman racked up the third longest suspension in NBA history. The six-game suspension came with a hefty price tag. Not only did the league fine Rodman $20,000, but frustrated Chicago Bulls officials withheld $182,926 of their problem player's pay covering the six games they were without his services.

Amazingly, Rodman's run-in with the ref was the third time he'd been suspended for head-butting. He had previously knocked noggins with Chicago Bulls forward Stacey King in 1992 and Utah Jazz guard John Stockton in 1994.

AFFRONT AND CENTER

Detroit Pistons center Bill Laimbeer called it quits in 1994, but not before literally leaving his mark on the NBA. The 6'11", 255-pound player hacked out a fine career, finishing at the lofty number-eight spot on the league's list of all-time foulers. Laimbeer was whistled a whopping 3,633 times during his fifteen-year career. Basher Bill accepted his role as the man the fans loved to hate, but the Piston proved to be an equal opportunity hacker. When he wasn't slamming opposing players who dared drive the lane, Laimbeer was tuning up on his teammates. In 1993, Detroit's 11-time All-Star Isiah Thomas broke his right hand slugging Laimbeer in practice! The 6'1" guard had grown tired of the burly center's rough play and threw a punch at his head. The blow didn't do much harm to Laimbeer, but it did cause Thomas to miss a month of play because of a fractured hand. Thomas should have known better than to brawl with Bill. During one particularly rough pre-season practice, he suffered a broken rib after coming within range of a Laimbeer elbow.

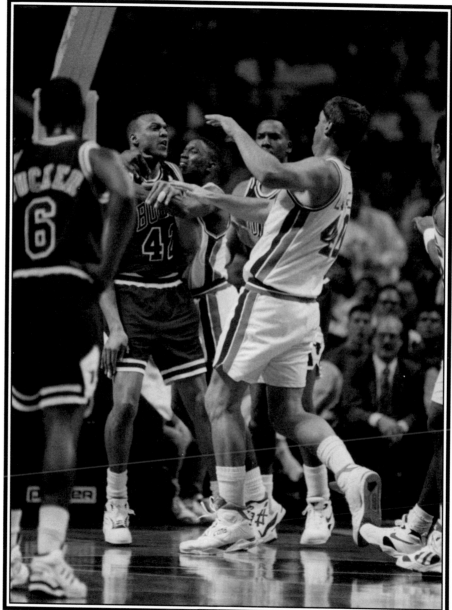

BILL LAIMBEER AND SCOTT WILLIAMS
TRYING TO FIGURE OUT THE TANGO.

AP/Wide World

CRIME SPRE

While most hoopster bad boys can at least wait until there's a game, Golden State Warriors guard Latrell "Spre" Sprewell made some head-turning headlines with an assault on Warriors Coach P. J. Carlesimo during a practice session on December 1, 1997. When Carlesimo unleashed his temper with taunts at Latrell, the 6'5", 190-pound Sprewell got himself kicked out of practice by attempting to strangle the coach . . . no word on whether the taunts included "Choke!" Some 15 minutes later, the basket(ball) case stormed back into practice, punching Carlesimo and threatening to kill him. Although the Warriors terminated Sprewell's $32-million contract and the NBA banned him for one year, Sprewell quickly regained the respect of all Americans by hiring O.J. attorney Johnnie Cochran to represent him in his bid for reinstatement. Definitely a novel take on the phrase, "Basketball's Dream Team," but every good player knows the meaning of a strong defense.

BEWILDER-RINK BRAWL

Detroit Piston Isiah Thomas apparently mistook the Palace of Auburn Hills for Joe Louis Arena during a game against the Chicago Bulls on April 12, 1993. When Chicago's Scott Williams and Detroit's Bill Laimbeer got into a scuffle, Thomas incapacitated Scott Williams with the classic rinkster move of pulling an opponent's jersey over his head. Williams and Laimbeer were both ejected, and reportedly spent several confused minutes searching for the penalty box.

AP/Wide World

ISIAH THOMAS TRIES TO PULL SCOTT WILLIAMS' JERSEY OFF;
THEN HE'LL GET HIM TO SIGN IT.

FOUL SHOTS

• It's not unusual to see a U.S. Senator fighting for a bill, but on February 18, 1975, future-politician Bill Bradley of the New York Knicks adopted a resolution to rap Rick Barry of the Golden State Warriors. Dollar Bill desperately wanted to alter the face of his foe, a future

THEY CAN'T JUMP, BUT THEY CAN PUNCH.

UPI/Corbis-Bettmann

Hall of Famer. The ref risked life and limb to separate the 6'5" Bradley and the 6'7" Barry who squared off during the first quarter of the New York-Golden State game at Madison Square Garden. The match-up of NBA All-Stars proved to be more posturing than punching. Bradley went on to bigger things after retiring in 1977 and returning to his home state of New Jersey. The former Knick showed an obvious knack for politics and eventually rose to the respected role of U.S. Senator — and even considered a run for the ultimate title of President. When asked in 1992, how a presidential nominee should be selected, the Democrat declared: "Line them up and let them shoot jump shots from the top of the key!"

• Three players were ejected for fighting and a whopping 70 fouls were whistled when pro football players from Dallas and Houston took off the pads for a "friendly" game of basketball in 1970. It was a costly court decision for the Cowboys. They not only lost the smash-and-grab game, 86-84, but also lost the services of three key players for the following day's count-in-the-standings NFL contest. The bench-riding Cowboys were Ron (broken nose) Widby, Walt (blackened eye) Garrison, and Dennis (groin pull) Homan.

• After scoring two of his career-high 36 points in a 1993 NBA playoff game, Reggie Miller of the Indiana Pacers smugly told front-row fans, "I just can't stop myself." However,

John Starks of the opposing New York Knicks did find a way to temporarily stop the man he'd been assigned to guard. He hauled off and head-butted the braggart. For mugging Miller, Starks was slapped with a flagrant foul, an ejection and a hefty fine.

• Irv Hairston may be the only college basketball player ever to leave a game in handcuffs. Hairston was a reserve guard for New Mexico State when the team dropped a heated 1983 game to Drake, 75-73. After the final buzzer sounded in Des Moines, Iowa, Hairston took some extra shots at the happy hometown fans. Before words could turn to whacks, concerned cops cuffed the guard and escorted him to a first-aid room. Hairston cooled down and was released.

> ## "I THREW A LEFT HOOK, BUT I WAS BACKPEDALING SO FAST IT NEVER GOT THERE."
>
> *— Baltimore Bullets center Bob Ferry, recalling*
> *a fight with Wilt Chamberlain*

FOULEST OF ALL

- It took less than half of the first quarter of a 1956 NBA game for Syracuse Nationals guard Dick Farley to hack himself a place in league history. It didn't even take Farley a full five minutes to bag the six-foul limit. The half-dozen hacks earned the 6'4", 190-pound player a prime spot on the Syracuse bench for the remainder of the game and, more importantly, a No. 1 listing in the NBA record book as the player to foul out the fastest! Over his three-year career, Farley was a bit overly physical, accumulating more fouls (429) than assists (386) in 211 games.

- On November 24, 1949, Syracuse slugged it out with the Anderson Packers to set the record for most total fouls (122). The starters from both teams fouled out during the five-overtime free-for-all won by Syracuse 125-123. The refs were whistle-weary after calling 56 fouls on the Nationals and a shameful 66 more on the Packers.

- While battling with the Baltimore Bullets on November 15, 1952, Syracuse was flagged for 60 fouls and set a single-team record for the most players to foul out in a game.

Amazingly, the officials allowed some of the disqualified to play on — because without them, the Nationals couldn't put five players on the court!

• In 1954, basketbrawlers from West Virginia high schools Weston and Grafton teamed up to commit a bruising 110 personal fouls. The squad from Weston was whistled for a whopping 59 team fouls, while the guys from Grafton got away with a mere 51 infractions during the wild, full-contact contest.

• Referees handed out a record 15 technical fouls during a brawl-marred basketball game between Chapman and Mansfield Colleges in 1990. Chapman led 73-60 with just 44 seconds remaining, when a pair of players got into a shoving match that quickly escalated into a full-court fiasco as both benches emptied. Eight players from Chapman and another seven from Mansfield were slapped with technicals. Mansfield converted 14 of their 16 free throws. However, Chapman made good on nine of their 14 penalty shots to win 82-74.

• There was a foul air in the gymnasium when the women's basketball team from Rutgers-Newark met intra-state rival Rutgers-Camden in 1993. A total of 59 fouls were whistled, resulting in 10 players hitting the showers early. Rutgers-Newark trailed 70-68 with 4:52 remaining in double overtime, yet won the game by forfeit when Rutgers-Camden had just one player left on the court!

• After whistling 49 fouls and six technical fouls, whistle-weary refs had seen enough of the high school girls basketball game in Vero Beach, Florida. There was 1:18 remaining in overtime when the exhausted officials called it a game, with St. Edward's leading Lincoln Park Academy 35-31. The peacekeepers were particularly peeved by the unruly players who were overturning chairs at courtside to protest calls and by Lincoln Park coach Malina Mack who refused to leave the gym following her second technical foul.

WOODY HAYES, NON-PARTISAN PUGILIST.

Chapter 4

LEADERS OF THE WHACK

WOODY HAYMAKERS

During his legendary stint at Ohio State University, feisty football coach Woody Hayes guided his Big Ten Buckeyes to plenty of wins. But it was his fiery temper that set the tone for his rough-and-tumble tenure on the Buckeye sidelines. Hot-headed Hayes was known to get physical with Ohio State players. But on December 29, 1978, the loco coach lashed out on national television against an opposing player. Hayes' behavior was way out of bounds when he sucker-punched Clemson University linebacker Charlie Bauman during the 1978 Gator Bowl in Jacksonville, Florida. Not only did the ABC-TV cameras capture the

> "IT WORRIES ME THAT THERE'S SUPPOSED TO BE TWO COACHES MEANER THAN I AM. I WOULD HATE TO HAVE THEM START REFERRING TO ME AS 'GOOD OLD WOODY.'"
>
> — *Woody Hayes*

unprovoked assault, they also zoomed in on wildman Woody as he threw a punch at Ohio offensive guard Ken Fritz, who was attempting to restrain his out-of-control coach.

Hayes is best-remembered for his hard-nosed, no-nonsense style at OSU. But Woody was known to sneak in some humor now and then when meeting the press. Once, while recruiting a Czechoslovakian kicker, Hayes noted: "During the eye examination, the doctor asked if he could read the bottom line of the chart. Well, the Czech kicker answered: 'Read it? Heck, I know him!'"

HALL OF SHAME

Woody wasn't the only coach to ever deliver a hard hit on an opposing player. Ed Hall, college football coach at Fairfield (Connecticut) University, actually made a touchdown-saving tackle during a 1978 game against Western New England College. Hall's Fairfield squad was holding onto a slim 15-14 lead when WNEC running back Jim Brown broke loose down the sideline for what looked like an easy score. At least until Hall leaped onto the field and decked the stunned runner. The officials didn't waste time awarding a touchdown to WNEC, which went on to win despite Fairfield's extra tackler.

BILLY BRAWL

When it comes to players or coaches who would rather settle disagreements with their fists rather than finesse, there are few that can compare to major league baseball's Billy Martin. The scrappy infielder, who rose to prominence with the New York Yankees, got into countless scrapes — on and off the playing field. On August 4, 1960, Martin let his clenched

UPI/Corbis-Bettmann

BILLY "BOTH FEET OFF THE GROUND" MARTIN
WALLOPS CUBS PITCHER JIM BREWER.

> ## "LOTS OF PEOPLE LOOK UP TO BILLY MARTIN. THAT'S BECAUSE HE JUST KNOCKED THEM DOWN."
>
> — *Major league pitcher Jim Bouton*

fingers do the talking when he delivered a roundhouse right to the face of Chicago pitcher Jim Brewer. The punch from the Cincinnati Reds slugger sent the Cubs hurler to the hospital with a broken bone near his right eye. Martin argued that Brewer deserved to be decked because he had dared pitch him too close! During successful stints as skipper of the New York Yankees, Oakland A's and Minnesota Twins, Martin perfected an aggressive style of play that became known as Billy Ball. However, he continued to rely on Billy Brawl to duke it out over disputes. Martin's best-known battles involved Yankees superstar and baseball Hall of Famer Reggie Jackson (in the dugout) and a marshmallow salesman (in an elevator). While managing the Texas Rangers, Martin armed himself with a baseball bat when Cleveland fans triggered a ninth-inning riot by storming the playing field in an attempt to attack Texas outfielder Jeff Burroughs. While Texas players came to the defense of their outmanned outfielder, the fearless leader defended their dugout. In fact, Martin broke his bat by repeatedly banging it against the dugout roof to drive back the attacking Indian fans. The June 4, 1974, fiasco also included a fireworks display — launched by short-fused fans in the direction of the Ranger dugout! Things got so bad that the officials handed Billy's beleaguered squad a forfeit win and got security to whisk the Texas players to safety. When managing the Oakland Athletics in 1981, Martin stepped out of the dugout during a game with the Minnesota Twins at Metropolitan Stadium — and was immediately pelted with hundreds of marshmallows. The soft, sugary treats were hurled by Twins fans to remind their former manager of his celebrated 1980 brawl with a marshmallow salesman.

KNIGHT OF THE LIVING DREAD

The demeanor of the dean of NCAA Division I basketball coaches has historically been Knight and day. During his 30-plus years at Indiana University, Bobby Knight has headed his Hoosiers through the best of times — a 32-0 record and the NCAA championship in 1976 — and the worst of times. Among the many Knightmares: A curse-filled postgame outburst at the 1995 NCAA tournament cost Indiana University $30,000 — despite the fund-raising efforts of a local DJ. Indiana alumnus Adam Smasher used the WNAP airwaves to urge fellow IU grads to chip in a measly buck each to bail out bad boy Bobby. Smasher was crushed when his passionate plea for donations raised a sickly three-week total of $167.

THE FEELING IS MUTUAL.

UPI/Corbis-Bettmann/Robin Jerstad

• During a 1994 game, Knight head-butted Hoosier player Sherron Wilkerson, who he'd been screaming at on the bench. The previous year, the crazed coach keyed on Indiana player Patrick Knight, his son. Whether or not Knight kicked his son or merely his son's chair didn't matter to horrified Hoosier officials who suspended the controversial coach for one game. Ironically, it was the mock whipping of IU forward Calbert Cheaney at the 1992 NCAA West Regionals that netted Knight the most knocks. But when a number of black leaders expressed offense over the incident, Bobby responded with surprise — and said he felt sorry for anyone who saw his silly stunt as a racial issue rather than a prank in poor taste.

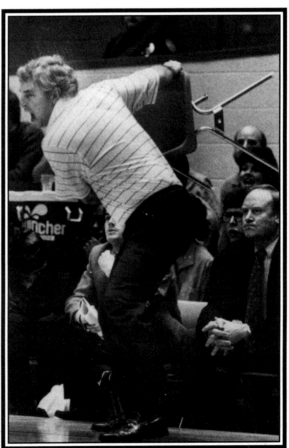

AP/Wide World

PERFECT FORM . . .

• The Indiana coach has had plenty of bad Knight moves, but perhaps his most famous foul-up occurred in 1985 when he tossed a chair across the basketball court during a game with Purdue. The foolish fling earned Knight an immediate ejection and a one-game suspension. The Hoosier head-case did issue an apology — because the chair he had launched nearly struck fans seated in the courtside wheelchair section.

AP/Wide World

BUT KNIGHT WILL HAVE TO CONVERT THE TOUGH SEVEN-TEN SPLIT WITH HIS SECOND CHAIR.

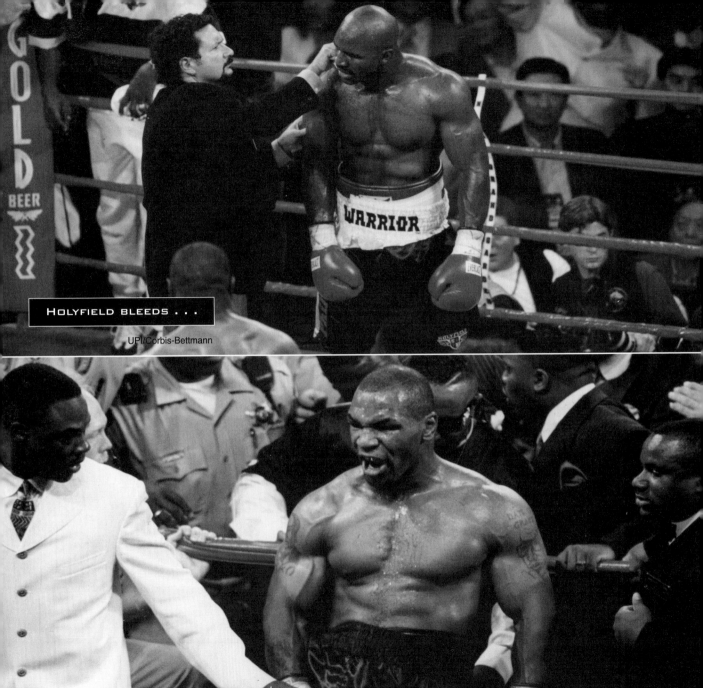

HOLYFIELD BLEEDS . . .

UPI/Corbis-Bettmann

TYSON SNARLS.

UPI/Corbis-Bettmann

Chapter 5

BRAWLS WITH A RING TO 'EM

BITE OF THE CENTURY

It was once bitten, twice eeeeyyyiiii! when heavyweight champ Evander Holyfield had both his ears pierced by heavyweight chomp Mike Tyson during their heavily hyped rematch on June 28, 1997. Holyfied lost a chunk of his right ear, but he did retain his WBA title when ref Mills Lane disqualified Tyson for chews-ing to bite rather than fight his opponent. Tyson was warned after he first sank his teeth into Holyfield's left ear during a third-round clinch. Lane stopped the big-bucks Las Vegas bout and ordered the judges to subtract two points from Tyson's scorecard. Round Four was barely under way when Tyson was disqualified for double-nibbling. The much-deserved DQ came a bit too late for Holyfield, who needed the bout like he needed another hole in his head. And that's just what he got — a nasty notch out of his ragged right ear! The Nevada Boxing Commission later took a big bite out of Tyson's $30-million purse — and banned the two-bit boxer from returning to the ring for a full ear . . . er, year.

Iron Mike's outrageous actions were hard to swallow. However, dental hijnks have always played a painful part in the world's greatest sports brawls:

• For instance, an overzealous rugby player was whacked with a six-month jail sentence in 1985 because he opened his mouth — and bit off the ear of an opponent! The gnashing New Zealander named Latu Vaeno definitely bit off more than he should've chewed. Rugby is a rough sport, but league officials wouldn't hear of any penalty less than a half-year ban — to be served behind bars — for the lout-mouthed Latu.

• A year later, Quebec forward Jimmy Mann did his bit to help his Nordiques win the 1986 National Hockey League playoff series with the Hartford Whalers. During a Game 2 rhubarb, mighty-mouth Mann sank his teeth into the cheek of Hartford player Torrie Robertson who immediately changed his team's nickname from Whalers to Wailers. The chomp was so deep, team docs sent Robertson for a tetanus shot. Meanwhile, the mad Mann was ordered to bite his time in the penalty box.

MOTHER OF ALL BRAWLS

Overprotective parent Minna Wilson made sure her son Tony was a "shoe-in" to win his 1989 light-heavyweight boxing bout against Steve McCarthy. Overmatched Tony was taking a beating from McCarthy before his mad-as-hell mom leaped into action. In the blink of an eye, the mano a mano match-up was transformed into a two-against-one tussle that would have made Hulk Hogan proud. The London crowd roared as Mother Wilson climbed into the ring, removed one of her shoes and began bonking her son's opponent on the head! Minna was quickly corralled by the ring official, but the damage was done. The well-heeled hits had left their mark on McCarthy's mug, bloodying the fighter's face so badly that British Boxing Board officials had no other choice but to call a halt to the bizarre bout. McCarthy was mugged a second time when the referee raised the arm of Wilson — Tony, not Minna — in victory!

BOWE KNOWS BRAWLING!

On July 11, 1996, heavyweight boxer Riddick Bowe "rang up" a controversial victory over hard-charging challenger Andrew Golota, who was disqualified for delivering repeated low blows. The bout held at New York's Madison Square Garden was exciting while it lasted, but the in-ring action was just a prelim to the chaos that erupted once the official decision was announced. In a flash, the frenzied followers of both fighters were engaged in hand-to-hand combat. It was during the mid-ring melee that Golota received perhaps his hardest blow of the night — an ear-ringing blast to the head with a portable phone wielded by a member of Bowe's entourage. The cheap-shot culprit was easy to collar. The blind-side blast was caught on video, resulting in police charges for the bell-ringer and sanctions against both camps. By year's end, a Bowe-Golota rematch was arranged. Amazingly, that heavily-hyped bout was also cut short as Golota was again disqualified for landing low blows to Bowe. But this time there was no post-fight phone fracas for the loser.

AP/Wide World/Ron Frehm

NO BOXERS VISIBLE, BUT PLENTY OF ACTION IN THE RING.

• Trouble seemed to follow Bowe. He won a 1991 bout over Elijah Tillery in a fight that more closely resembled a wrestling match. The actual fight lasted just one round as both boxers ignored the bell and launched into a wild free-for-all that included kicks and choke holds! At one point, Tillery, who was disqualified for battering Bowe with a series of flagrant kicks, was dragged by the neck up and over the top rope by Bowe's mad-as-hell manager, Rock Newman. It took District of Columbia police 10 minutes to restore order at the Capital Center.

• During a 1994 fight, Bowe stooped to a new low when he floored Buster Mathis Jr., with a rocking right to the head. Unfortunately, Mathis was clearly down on one knee when Bowe blasted him into la la land with the illegal fourth-round blow. Bad boy Bowe was spared a disqualification when fight officials opted instead for a "no contest" ruling.

STREET FIGHTIN' MAD

On April 7, 1991, former heavyweight champion Larry Holmes began a boxing comeback with a wild doubleheader that rocked Hollywood, Florida. In his first fight of the day, Holmes

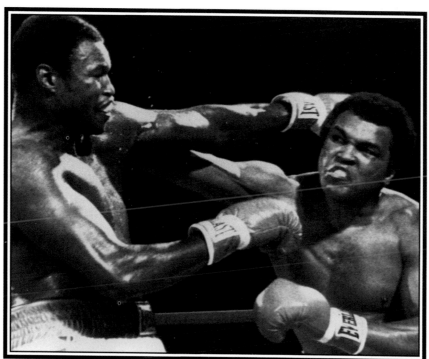

HOLMES AND ALI — GUYS WHO COULD BRAWL WITH THE BEST OF THEM.

scored an easy victory, clubbing club fighter Tim "Doc" Anderson — his only scheduled challenger. But then Larry lost plenty of points for class by engaging in an embarrassing encore. The once-respected ring master began battling it out in the street with heavyweight boxer Trevor Berbick, who'd been heckling him from ringside throughout the Anderson bout. Showing more moves than he had earlier in the ring, Holmes chased Berbick through the parking lot, scaling cars filled with fight fans who'd come to relive memories of this once-classy champion. But the man who took the title from The Greatest, Muhammad Ali, was now denting their respect . . . not to mention their cars! The Holmes-Berbick bout was a fierce free-swinging affair for the few minutes before police arrived and put an end to the shameful Punch-Out in the Parking Lot — hardly the Thrilla in Manilla.

BOXER SHORTS

• Spanish fighter Valentin Loren was hit with a lifetime ban from amateur boxing following his outrageous actions during a featherweight bout at the 1964 Olympics. After repeated warnings from the ref about "holding" and "hitting with an open glove," Loren was disqualified. But the boxer wasn't about to quit throwing punches — he turned to Hungarian referee Gyorgy Sermer and slugged him square on the jaw.

• Mayhem erupted during a preliminary boxing match at the 1924 Olympics when referee T. H. Walker disqualified Italian welterweight Antonio Oldania for holding his opponent. As the flustered fighter slumped to the canvas and began sobbing, his incensed supporters began pelting Walker with sticks, coins and other debris. The assailed referee escaped serious injury thanks to a small army of American, British and South African boxers who rushed to the ring and surrounded Walker, escorting him to safety.

• The 1940 welterweight match between Fritzie Zivac and Al "Bummer" Davis ended in a brawl — with the police. The referee stepped in and disqualified Davis after the fighter delivered his tenth foul blow. However, both boxers ignored the bout-ending bell and continued slugging it out at center ring. It took a small army of cornermen and cops to stop the slugfest.

• Superwelterweight champ Terry Norris lost his title in 1994 when he was disqualified for slugging challenger Luis Santana on the back of his head. It was déjà vu all over again when the fighters met again five months later. Norris, a 13-1 favorite, dominated Santana over the first three rounds of the rematch. But the much better boxer blew it again when he landed a lights-out punch well after the round-ending bell sounded. Santana was being carted from the ring on a stretcher when the ringside announcer declared him the winner — once again — via disqualification.

• Heavyweight boxer Willie Richardson was so keyed up during the pre-fight introductions he began swinging wildly at his unprepared opponent Roger Rischer before their 1965 bout. Apparently enjoying the moment, the fighter also flailed away at his opponent's handlers. Ringside judges cancelled the bout before it officially began.

DOES MANAGER DAVEY JOHNSON KNOW WHAT'S COMING?

Chapter 6

A REF WAY
TO MAKE A LIVING

ILLEGAL SPITTER

Baltimore Orioles second baseman Roberto Alomar spit squarely in the eye of sportsmanship when he spit in the face of American League umpire John Hirschbeck on September 27, 1996. The juicy outburst by the All-Star infielder was an ugly exclamation point to the jawing Alomar gave Hirschbeck following his ouster from a late-season game in Toronto. The home plate ump angered Alomar first by calling him out on strikes — on a pitch that appeared outside the strike zone — and then by giving the outraged Oriole the thumb for the crude comments he had called out from the dugout. Both Alomar and Baltimore manager Davey Johnson raced to home plate to confront Hirschbeck. Alomar was being restrained by his teammates when he opened his mouth and let loose with the stream of spit that caught the official on the kisser. American League president Gene Budig quickly handed down a five-game suspension — to be served not during Baltimore's upcoming playoff series with the Cleveland Indians, but at the start of the 1997 season! The spit hit the fan as baseball buffs from coast-to-coast booed the ruling, and the unionized major league umpires threatened to strike the post-season playoffs. Amazingly, all feuding parties kissed and made up, and the show went on with Alomar turning hero again by blasting a 12th-inning homer to beat Cleveland 4-3 and lead Baltimore to a 3-1 series crown in the American League Championship.

MAD ABOUT BLUE

The "honor" of being the first female to officiate a professional baseball game belongs to New Yorker Bernice Gera who weathered three years of litigation to fulfill her dream. The much-beleaguered woman in blue finally made sports history on June 24, 1972, when she strolled onto the ballfield to make calls during a minor league doubleheader between home host Geneva (NY) Mets and the Auburn Phillies. Alas, poor Bernice was quick to discover that diamonds aren't always a girl's best friend. Gera stood her ground as fans shouted words of discouragement and players and coaches from both teams questioned her calls — especially the ouster of Auburn coach Nolan Campbell. But it was one and

FIRST-TIME UMPIRE GERA TAKES A LITTLE HEAT.

done for the flustered official, who had fallen victim to the "brawl boys network" better known as Major League Baseball. Shortly after the final out of the first game was barked out, Gera made the most difficult decision of her fledgling career. She called it quits and walked off the field — and into the history books.

JUDGE MENTALS

Boxing referee Keith Walker found himself in the fight of his life at the 1988 Summer Olympics in Seoul, South Korea. The no-nonsense New Zealander was forced to fight his way out of the boxing ring and then the jam-packed arena after he sparked a near-riot with

REFEREE WALKER SEEKS SHELTER IN A STORM.

his scoring decision that floored any medal chances of the South Korean competitor. A heart-beat after Walker raised the arm of the victorious boxer, the outraged audience morphed into an angry mob, roaring their disapproval, flinging cups and programs — and menacingly making their way toward the ringed-in referee. But there was an even more imminent threat to Walker's well-being. In a flash, several of the South Korean's crazed cornermen had climbed through the ring ropes and were intent on pounding some sense into the outnumbered official. Walker was treated like a punching bag before he broke free of the lynch mob and made a beeline for an arena door. Hard blows were landed by at least three cornermen, a trainer, a fight judge and a security guard paid to protect against such violence. The shameful scene was witnessed by millions of TV viewers worldwide.

OFFICIAL BUSINESS

• Visiting soccer official Constantine Fatouros found himself in a helluva jam following a heated match in 1965. Fanatical fans on the island of Chios sought to avenge their home team's loss by lynching the Greek referee. For a moment, it looked like frightened Fatouros didn't have a prayer. But then he stumbled upon a tailor-made disguise — a priest's garb complete with a head-covering cassock. The disguise proved divine for Fatouros, who slipped away from Chios and the revenge-minded mob of sore losers.

• It's usually a pitcher rather than an umpire who gets "knocked out" of a baseball game. But during a 1970 Texas League game, home plate ump Nick Emeterio was kayoed by Dallas-Fort Worth pitcher Greg Arnold. The hot-headed hurler threw the haymaker after Emeterio charged him with a balk. For throwing the illegal one-hitter, Arnold was knocked out of action for the remainder of the season by league officials.

• In 1992, Oakland manager Tony LaRussa grabbed a bat and furiously charged from the A's dugout in the direction of home plate umpire Greg Kosc. LaRussa was livid over the "strike three" call from Kosc that sent Oakland outfielder Rickey Henderson back to the

> **"I'VE BEEN MOBBED, CUSSED, BOOED, KICKED IN THE ASS, PUNCHED IN THE FACE, HIT WITH MUDBALLS AND WHISKEY BOTTLES AND HAD EVERYTHING FROM SHOES TO FRUITS AND VEGETABLES THROWN AT ME. AN UMPIRE SHOULD HATE HUMANITY."**
>
> — *Major league baseball umpire Joe Rue*

bench with his bat on his shoulder. Luckily, the incensed skipper was restrained by his own players as well as members of the Milwaukee Brewers before he could get within striking distance of the man behind the plate. Kosc kept his cool during the chaos — and rerouted the burning-mad batman to the A's locker room.

• National League umpire James Lincoln was the target of so much on-field abuse during his 1913 debut, the major league baseball game proved to be his first and last game. The rookie ump triggered the onslaught by making a questionable call against the New York Giants. The players immediately began vilifying Lincoln's eyesight, jeering his judgment and even assailing his ancestry. But the worst was yet to come. After the final out was

> **"THE OLD FAN USED TO YELL, 'KILL THE UMPIRE!' THE NEW FAN TRIES TO DO IT."**
>
> — *Psychiatrist Arnold Beisser*

called, miffed members of the losing Giants surrounded the frightened official. They then shoved and spiked poor Lincoln, while all the while cursing his game-calling ability. The man in blue immediately bade farewell to baseball — but not before advising fellow ump Bill Klem, "It's a horrible business!"

• Umpire Bill Byron found himself in a real pickle after ejecting St. Louis Cardinal Art Butler from a 1915 major league baseball game. Wild Cardinal fans booed the ump and then pelted him with over 100 cucumbers! No one ever figured out why the fans were armed with the vegetables.

NOT TO WORRY . . . THE RIGHT CROSS IS LEGAL IN HOCKEY.

Chapter 7

THE GOON, THE BLADE AND THE ULFIE

THE BIG ULF

Mirror, mirror on the wall, who's the foulest of them all? When it comes to hard-hitting hockey, one of the all-time hated players has to be Ulf Samuelsson, who was proclaimed The Dirtiest Player in the NHL in 1996. His philosophy says it all. The rough-housing New York Ranger was so proud of his cheatin' art that he voted for himself in the *Sports Illustrated* dirtiest player poll. By collecting 27 of the 56 votes cast, Ulf easily outdistanced the second-place finisher, Bryan Marchment of the Edmonton Oilers, to earn the dishonorable honor. Cheap-shot Samuelsson, the man credited with cutting short the career of Boston great Cam Neely, is so despised by opponents that more than once he found himself on the wrong end of a sucker-punch. Such savage assaults were cheered by many and officials were often urged to reward rather than punish the puncher! Enforcer Tie Domi of the Toronto Maple Leafs took pride in his one-punch knockout of Samuelsson on October 14, 1995. But the NHL quickly iced Domi with an eight-game suspension. Through a combination of a stiff fine and lost salary, the out-of-line Maple Leaf skater was socked for $26,000.

> "IT'S REALLY SIMPLE. I'LL DO WHATEVER IT TAKES TO KEEP OPPOSING PLAYERS FROM PUTTING THE PUCK IN THE NET. SOMETIMES IT'S ILLEGAL."
>
> — *New York Rangers defenseman Ulf Samuelsson*

KINGS OF PAIN

The Los Angeles Kings and Edmonton Oilers punched up some pretty impressive numbers when they squared off for a penalty-plagued National Hockey League game on February 26, 1990. The action on the ice was far from nice, and the hard-hitting teams skated into the record book by combining for an amazing all-time high totalling 85 penalties — including 14 for fighting and 27 for roughing! When the final horn sounded, the whistle-weary officiating crew had socked the players almost as much as the players had socked each other. The penalty box seats never had a chance to cool as players collected a whopping 354 minutes of combined penalty time! The teams shattered the one-game mark for penalties, while the Oilers struck for an all-time single team record of 44.

FAST START

We don't puck around, hey! Before many of the fans had a chance to find their seats, the Edmonton Oilers and Calgary Flames had put down their sticks and put up their dukes, converting the skating rink into a boxing ring just 28 seconds after the game-opening face-off of a 1987 National Hockey League game. The three-man officiating crew could do little but steer clear of the glove-dropping, shirt-grabbing combatants, as five separate fights broke out among the visiting Edmonton and host Calgary hooligans. The first-period fisticuffs may have fired up the fans, but it also cut short the action for the dirty half-dozen players the officials sent packing once order was restored. The peeved peacekeepers were far from finished dishing out slapshots. By the time play resumed with 19:32 left in the first period, the men in stripes had sentenced the remaining rumblers to a whopping 108 minutes in the penalty box!

> ## "IF FIGHTS WERE FAKED, YOU WOULD SEE ME IN MORE OF THEM."
>
> — *New York Rangers right wing Rod Gilbert*

NO TENDER MERCIES

In 1987, Philadelphia Flyers rookie goalie Ron Hextall netted a previously unheard-of 104 penalty minutes — a total nearly double the recognized high for naughty net tenders in the NHL. The Philly fanatic was whistled six times for slashing, twice for high-sticking, once for roughing and once for leaving his post near the net to take part in a brawl. On several other occasions, Hextall drew delay of game penalties by intentionally driving the puck up over the rink's protective glass and into the crowd. Hextall's hot head was held in check for eight games in 1987 — while he served a suspension for slashing. The fiery

Flyer goalie was also sidelined for the first 12 games of the 1989-90 season. Hextall was handed the severe suspension after he attacked an opposing player during Philadelphia's final playoff game on May 11, 1989.

UPI/Corbis-Bettmann

REF GAUTHIER APPEARS TO BE SLIPPING
A STRAIGHTJACKET ONTO RON HEXTALL.

LIGHTS OUT

It was boom! boom! Out go the lights . . . yet on went the fights during the 1987 World Junior Hockey Championships match featuring Canada and the Soviet Union. The officiating crew was horribly outnumbered as fierce fisticuffs erupted over all patches of the arena ice. The worried refs were left in the dark over how to restore peace on ice as the deafening din from their shrill whistlings and shouted warnings went unheeded. Once he caught his breath, the desperate chief official ordered arena workers to turn off all the lights. But even the sudden darkness failed to dim the players' desire to punch out each other's lights. Once the fighting fizzled and order was restored, the refs retaliated. Banning both teams from further tournament play was only the beginning. Fearing another flare-up, the officials ordered the players to steer clear of the closing ceremonies and awards banquet.

DOOMS-DAVE

Ron Hextall's overly-aggressive play would have been a perfect fit 15 years earlier when Philadelphia was nicknamed "The Broad Street Bullies." Behind savage stickmen like Dave Schultz and slick scorers like captain Bobby Clarke, the Flyers notched back-to-back Stanley Cup championships in 1974 and 1975. Defenseman Dave Schultz fractured the NHL single-season record for penalty minutes when he banged out a whopping 472 over the '74-'75 season. He also held down the fourth spot on that very same list with 405 penalty minutes in '77-'78. And despite a relatively short nine-year career, Schultz holds the No. 12 spot in all-time penalty minutes. He spent 2,294 minutes in the penalty box during stints with Philly, Los Angeles, Pittsburgh and Buffalo! Schultz's shining moment occurred April 6, 1978. While playing for Pittsburgh, he collected nine penalties during a game at Detroit. The five minors, two majors and two 10-minute misconducts remain only one penalty shy of the NHL's all-time mark set by Boston's Chris Nilan on March 31, 1981.

AP/Wide World

OUCH! GOALIE GARY SMITH TAKES A HIT
FROM "THE HAMMER," DAVE SCHULTZ.

SLAP SHOTS

• Montreal Canadiens tough guy Chris Nilan once drew a misconduct penalty while he was already in the penalty box! It was during a 1981 hockey game that Nilan, who was supposed to be cooling his heels, hurled a puck at Pittsburgh Penguins defenseman Paul Baxter. The league tossed back a three-game suspension.

> **"WE'RE GOING TO HAVE TO DO SOMETHING ABOUT ALL THIS VIOLENCE OR PEOPLE ARE GOING TO KEEP ON BUYING TICKETS."**
>
> *— Toronto Maple Leafs owner Conn Smythe*

• No matter how you slice it, a hockey coach is better off remaining on the bench behind safety glass when a fight breaks out. New York Rangers coach and general manager Emile Francis learned that lesson in 1965 when he tore off his sports coat while leaping onto the ice to join a fray. The Rangers who followed Francis off the bench landed skates-first on their coach's jacket, slicing it to bits!

• It was a true bench-clearing hockey brawl when the Detroit Red Wings and Minnesota North Stars locked horns in 1985 — even the suit-wearing head coaches clashed. The players were duking it out near the Detroit bench when Minnesota's main man Glen Sonmor stunned the crowd by slipping onto the ice and making a baby-steps beeline to the other side. Upon reaching his destination, Sonmor started slugging it out with Red Wings coach Nick Polano. Once order was restored, Sonmor was ejected.

"A PUCK IS A HARD RUBBER DISK THAT HOCKEY PLAYERS STRIKE WHEN THEY CAN'T HIT ONE ANOTHER."

— *Sportswriter Jimmy Cannon*

• The figure skating competition at the 1956 Winter Olympics in Cortina d'Ampezzo, Italy, turned into an orange ice escapade. The event had to be stopped in mid-skate because the unruly crowd began pelting the competitors with oranges. Most of the fruit-flinging fans were incensed over the low scores the judges handed a popular pair of German skaters. The ice had to be cleared off three times before officials allowed the skaters to continue.

• Tony Blanda videotaped plenty of NHL games in 1986, then erased all the hockey action . . . but the brawling! The super fan of fighting soon became a celebrity throughout the United States and Canada for his videotaped violence edited down to 6,000 of the fiercest slugfests on ice. Blanda soon went from simply trading his tapes with friends to shipping copies all across North America. "It's a hobby . . . like stamps," noted the baron of beatings, obviously referring to the fact both pastimes involve lickings.

Eric Cantona seems to have made the papers.

Chapter 8
FIELD OF SCREAMS

ERIC THE DREAD

In 1995, soccer superstar Eric Cantona reacted to a taunt-filled tirade from the bleachers by charging off the field and into the stands where he beat the hell out of the offending fan. As would be expected from such a fleet-of-foot soccer star, Cantona kept his hands away from the offensive action. Instead, the fiery Frenchman battered the big-mouth with a swift series of well-aimed karate kicks. For his out-of-bounds actions, livid league officials booted Cantona off his Manchester United team and ordered him to perform 120 hours of community service. Cantona was crucified in the British press, but it wasn't long before he cashed in on his outrageous assault. Video-playing kids were soon getting a kick from "Fever Pitch Soccer: Bringing the Game into Disrepute." The game, which catered more to foul-minded contestants than those concerned with the ideals of fair play, starred a Cantona clone whose goal appeared to be barging into the bleachers and scoring with vicious karate kicks to the spectators.

DEAD WRONG

The world's worst soccer riot erupted May 24, 1964, in Lima, Peru, as the Peruvian national team was hosting the Argentinian national team to determine which South American squad would advance to play in Tokyo at the Summer Olympics. Investigators

THIS FAN PAYS FOR
HIS EXUBERANCE . . .

AP/Wide World

later determined that a wave of panic spurred the crowd of 45,000-plus to stampede for the stadium exits. The tragic crush which claimed 318 lives and left hundreds of the more fortunate fans injured but alive was sparked by a single crazed fan who rushed onto the field to protest a ref's ruling that wiped away a game-tying goal. Three policemen and an attack dog quickly collared the crazed fan, but the sight of such brutality enraged many spectators. The violence escalated to the point where the game was forgotten and the fans trampled each other while attempting to flee from the thick clouds of tear gas police released into the stadium.

The riot wasn't the first time the Peruvian fans lost control. Peru's national team withdrew from the 1936 Berlin Olympics after its soccer squad was ordered to replay a controversial 4-2 victory over Austria. A Jury of Appeals voided the game because Peruvian fans had stormed the field and assaulted an Austrian player. In the midst of the mayhem, Peru picked

MANY OTHERS WOULD PAY MORE DEARLY.

up a pair of quick goals. Since the final margin proved to be those two goals, officials proclaimed that the soccer match should be replayed — this time without fans in the stands. The pouting Peruvians packed up their gear and convinced their country's entire contingent of athletes to join them in an early exit from the games.

SHORT KICKS

• Brazilian soccer star Zico was handed a four-game suspension for unsportsmanlike behavior in the 1994 Japan Professional Soccer League championship series. Zico's dastardly deed? As the officials positioned the ball for a penalty kick by the opposition, Zico dared walk up and spit upon the ball.

• When the favored Brazilian soccer team was upset 1-0 by Argentina in a 1990 World Cup soccer match, their fans were outraged. Thousands of blame-toting crazies stormed the airport as the losing team arrived back home. Many of the angry fans demanded the head of coach Sebastiao Lazaroni. The frightened coach slipped out through a rear exit and hopped the first flight out of Brazil.

• Manchester United is one of the most popular soccer clubs in England. Unfortunately, Manchester's fans are popular, too — with the stadium security officers and local police who've responded to the wild wave of alcohol-induced acts of violence. The team added fuel to the fire in 1996 when it marketed its own brand of booze — Manchester United Premier Blend.

> "I'VE SAID IT TIME AND AGAIN, AND I KNOW THERE ARE MANY STUDENTS OF HUMAN BEHAVIOR WHO DISAGREE WITH ME. BUT, WITH MY CONSIDERABLE EXPERIENCE, I FEEL THE SAFEST AND MOST SATISFACTORY REACTION TO BEING FOULED IS BY RETALIATING WITH A PUNCH TO THE NOSE."
>
> — *NHL president Clarence Campbell*

• The 1992 video *Soccer's Hard Men* fondly recalled the dirty antics of brawling British legends such as Ron "Chopper" Harris and Norman "Bites Yer Legs" Hunter. Narration was handled by Wimbledon Dons midfielder Vinny Jones. Viewers were instructed on the most effective ways to foul an opponent, including eye poking, toe stomping, ear elbowing, testicles grabbing and cleat raking of the Achilles tendon! Football Association officials were so pained by the production they charged Jones with "bringing the game into disrepute."

• Italian police confiscated knives, rocks, clubs and helmets after stopping a six-bus convoy of French soccer fans in 1991. The 300 well-armed fans were en route to Milan for the European Champions Cup match between Italy's A.C. Milan and France's Olympique Marseille. Thanks to the cops, the squads played to a peaceful 1-1 tie.

• In 1993, 50 fans of Argentina's Chacarita Juniors soccer team were so determined to attend an away match, they hijacked a pair of public buses and forced the paying passengers to get off. The drivers were then instructed to forego their regular routes and head instead to Buenos Aires for the big game. The brazen bus hijackers managed to steer clear of immediate trouble by dragging along the drivers into the stadium — then ordering them to transport them back home after the match!

• Hooliganism ran so rampant during the 1991 Polish soccer season, league officials had a devil of a time keeping control of their rowdy fans. The frazzled front office of the second-ranked Wisla Krakow club went straight to the top for help. Free passes were dished out to dozens of priests-in-training attending a local seminary. The young men who showed up in their religious robes and collars were sprinkled throughout the stadium. The program proved to be the answer to the prayers of team officials.

• A European Champions Cup soccer match between Dynamo Dresden and Red Star Belgrade was suspended in 1991 when unruly fans began throwing rocks and bottles onto the field. But that was just the start of the fireworks that followed. Red Star was leading 2-1 when the field lit up like the Fourth of July and the players lit out for cover. Out of the bleachers came a fierce bombardment of firecrackers and bottle rockets! Riot police eventually doused the enthusiasm of the short-fused spectators, but only after they blasted back at the bleacher bombers with water cannons.

BRYAN PUCKERS UP.

Chapter 9

NATIONAL FOOTBRAWL LEAGUE

STRIFE OF BRYAN

Loose-cannon linebacker Bryan Cox proved to be every bit as good at making trouble as he was at making tackles when he joined the Miami Dolphins in 1991. Cox collected many unsportsmanlike conduct penalties after losing his cool. But his biggest bonehead move took place at Buffalo's Rich Stadium on December 17, 1995. With two minutes remaining in the important intra-conference game, Cox was sacked by officials for brawling with Bills fullback Carwell Gardner. The disqualified Dolphin player was literally spittin' mad as he was escorted off the field by stadium security. In full view of everyone, Bryan brazenly spit at the booing Bills fans seated nearest to the end zone tunnel. The disgusting display drew the deranged Dolphin a $17,500 fine from livid league officials who said "rubbish" to Cox's argument that his outrageous actions were aimed at the Buffalo fans who were dousing him with beer and trash. The Dolphins lost the game, 23-20, and then Cox, who signed with the Chicago Bears as a free agent on February 21, 1996.

Along with his Pro Bowl play, Cox left Miami with plenty of bad memories. In 1993, he was fined $10,000 for making a "flip" gesture to the fans in Buffalo. The week prior to his shameful spitting exhibition, Cox made all the sports shows by cussing up a storm after the Dolphins squeaked by Kansas City, 21-20. The defender took his tantrums to Chicago where he was whacked with an $85,000 fine for making an obscene gesture to an official. Through his first four seasons in the NFL, belligerent Bryan had been fined eight times for a total of $123,000.

COLLEGE CHAMPIONS

• When it comes to brawling, practice makes perfect. Members of the University of Miami Hurricanes concluded a 1991 pre-season practice game by kicking off a wild on-field fight. The inter-squad squabble erupted over turf — the "orange" team didn't appreciate members of the "white" team running through their practice area. Once the Hurricanes' ill winds subsided, local sports scribes had their say. "The brawl was the only part of their game that was in mid-season form," said *Miami Herald* reporter Dan LeBatard.

> "THERE'S NOTHING THAT CLEANSES YOUR SOUL LIKE GETTING THE HELL KICKED OUT OF YOU."
>
> — *Woody Hayes*

• In 1991, University of Miami defensive lineman Mark Caesar became the first football player arrested at Florida State University's Doak Campbell Stadium in Tallahassee. The hulking 290-pound Hurricane was collared by campus cops and charged with a misdemeanor for soaking Seminole fans with ice water following Miami's dramatic 17-16 victory. "The fans were being abusive so I retaliated and threw some ice back," Caesar argued.

FANDEMONIUM!

When it came to playing smash-mouth professional football, Baltimore linebacker Mike Curtis was true blood-and-guts tough while roving the middle of the playing field for the Colts during the early 1970s. The savage defender known as "Mad Dog" had boiled his

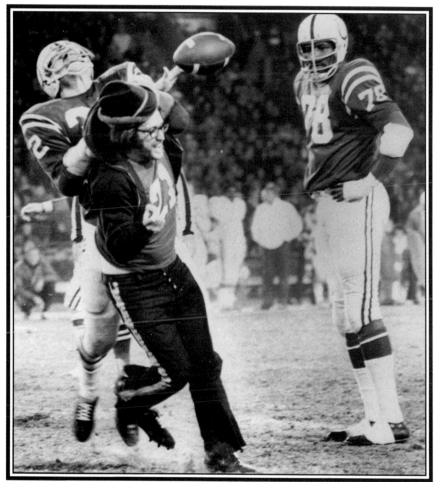

"JEEZ . . . I WAS JUST KIDDING AROUND."

game down to one simple rule — inflict heavy hurtin' on anyone who dared pick up the ball and run in his direction. One special moment of mayhem occurred on December 11, 1971, when a foolhardy fan ran out onto the Baltimore field during a break in the action. More brave than smart, the trespasser playfully scooped up the ball and took off running. Most of the host Colts and visiting Miami Dolphins stood by and watched, but not Mad Dog. Curtis took exception to the intruder and smashed him to the turf with a single bone-breaking blow. "I knocked him down, not to hurt him, but to knock him down, get the ball back and get rid of his rear end, period," he later said. "I didn't think it was a joke that I was working out there. A lot of other guys might think that it's funny to see a fan run out on the football field, to me it was my job."

SAD SACKS

• Curses! The Dubuque (Iowa) Spartans forfeited a 1952 college football game by a bizarre 1-0 score — and the blame belonged solely on the head of their foul-mouthed coach. Dubuque was trailing Iowa Wesleyan 7-0 when a couple of controversial fourth-quarter calls spurred Spartan coach Moco Mercer into a potty-mouthed protest. Mercer spewed obscenities at referee Fran DeReus until the head official tired of his sideline serenade. DeReus interrupted the crazed coach's tirade just long enough to scoop up the game ball, trot off the field — and announce to the crowd "The game is forfeited!"

• Detroit Lions defensive tackle Alex Karras had such poor eyesight that he once beat up his own brother during a 1962 NFL game. Tired of the continual holding by Chicago Bears tackle Stan Jones, Karras decided to teach his opponent a lesson. On the very next snap, Karras charged across the line of scrimmage, unleashed a couple of hard punches, then delivered one swift kick for good measure. Unfortunately, the player being pummeled wasn't Jones — it was Alex's older brother, Ted. Karras hadn't seen Chicago pull the switch just prior to the snap.

> "I WOULDN'T EVER SET OUT TO HURT ANYBODY DELIBERATELY UNLESS IT WAS, YOU KNOW, IMPORTANT — LIKE A LEAGUE GAME OR SOMETHING."
>
> — *Chicago Bears linebacker Dick Butkus*

SHARKIE, OF THE SAN JOSE SHARKS, AND STANLEY C. PANTHER,
OF THE FLORIDA PANTHERS, MAKE MASCOT MAYHEM.

AP/Wide World/John Dunn

Chapter 10
MASCOTS IN A JAM

OWL! THAT HURTS!

The feathers flew when the costumed mascots for cross-town rivals Temple and St. Joseph's got into a major flap during a 1994 college basketball game in Philadelphia. The bird-brained combatants — the Temple Owl and the St. Joseph's Hawk — locked claws as their respective schools hooped it up on the court. On this nasty night, there were no signs of brotherly love between the taloned twosome. But as the birds flew into action, all heads turned away from the court for a birds-eye view of the boxing wing. The tussle between these plucky pugilists quickly migrated into a full-scale melee which involved both players and cheerleaders alike. In a city where Rocky once ruled the ring, the Owl and the Hawk pecked out their own piece of history by squaring off for one unforgettable squawk. Emotions were flying high as more and more people came out to fray. Once order on the court was restored, officials determined it was the Temple Owl who-o-o, who-o-o was to blame for ruffling the Hawk's feathers and sparking the wild melee. The costumed characters were screeching out their usual game-time taunts when the Owl threw a "fake punch" which separated the Hawk from his huge head. After both of the beaked brawlers were shooed from courtside, Owl-less Temple went on to ground Hawk-less St. Joseph's, 76-64.

HAWK AND SHOVE

Another flap that made the feathers fly from the St. Joseph's Hawk took place in Philadelphia in 1988. The intra-city college contest between the St. Joe's and LaSalle basketball teams was marred by a mascot-triggered bench-clearing brawl — that broke out between the cheerleaders! LaSalle's female cheerleaders were performing a dance routine when the St. Joe's Hawk flew to midcourt and began shaking his feathers alongside them. LaSalle's male cheerleaders didn't appreciate the bird sticking his beak into their business, so they grabbed the costumed critter and tried to carry him off the court. The stubborn trespasser refused to fly, but plenty of fists did. Now it was the St. Joe's cheerleaders' turn to charge from the sidelines and do battle for their big bird. The brawl, which was full of peppy punches and cheers from the pumped-up crowd, raged at center court until officials enlisted players from both teams to clear the combatants.

COSTUME BRAWLS

• Auburn's War Eagle mascot went on the attack when University of Florida receiver Wes Chandler dared score a touchdown during a 1976 college football game. The stunned player had just entered the Auburn end zone and was about to celebrate his TD when the angry Eagle landed upon him in a flurry of feathers. As Chandler frantically fought off the big bird, the referee flagged Auburn with a 15-yard penalty for "illegal participation by the mascot." Florida overcame the bird-brained behavior and beat Auburn, 24-19.

• Harvey Wallbanger, the 1,500-pound bison mascot of the Arizona Rattlers, knocked linebacker Richard Ashe out of his team's 1993 Arena Football League home opener. Team officials were buffaloed into believing it was a great idea for huge Harvey to charge across the field whenever the Rattlers struck for a touchdown. But following a third-quarter score against the Detroit Drive, the massive mascot trampled Ashe during its sideline-to-sideline celebratory stampede.

> ## "IF THEY TOOK AWAY OUR STICKS AND GAVE US BROOMS, WE'D STILL HAVE FIGHTS."
>
> *-New York Rangers center Phil Esposito*

• A bench-clearing brawl that broke out at the 1993 World Hockey Championships featured players from Germany and France — and a huge penguin that waddled onto the ice and into the fray. Inside the black-and-white bird costume was Sven Kielmann, who was being paid to mingle with the fans in his role as event mascot. But Sven stuck his beak where it didn't belong. Luckily the costume was well-padded because the peacekeeping penguin was bonked on the beak with a hockey stick. The mauled mascot made it through the melee, then took one look at his bashed-in beak and noted: "I'm glad it wasn't my own head."

CALE YARBOROUGH LOOKS TO BE HAVING A VERY BAD HAIR DAY . . .

AND HE'S JUST NOT HAPPY ABOUT IT.

Chapter 11

MISCEL-ZANIEST

LAPS OF SANITY

Let's hear it for the good ol' boys of brawling! The nation's most-respected racing circuit, NASCAR, has quite a checkered past when it comes to members cruisin' for bruisin's. For all the fast and furious action they've provided fans on the circular circuit, these motor-mouthed men have added plenty of off-track action with their adrenalin-fueled fiascoes. Revved-up racers Cale Yarborough and the Brothers Allison — Donnie and Bobby — took part in perhaps the sport's most famous fight. The legendary drivers became fast enemies at the 1979 Daytona 500 when Donnie Allison "bumped" Yarborough during the final lap, putting both cars out of action. Soon there would be quite a row near pit row as both men overheated and began wrestling on the hot asphalt track. The race crowd roared as Bobby Allison zoomed to his brother's side to battle Yarborough — a veteran alligator wrestler!

• During qualifying runs at the North Wilkesboro (North Carolina) Speedway in 1993, Ricky Rudd and Brett Bodine brawl. The skirmish comes two weeks after the drivers collided at another track. Rudd sucker punches Bodine after smiling and congratulating him on a good run. "He scuffed me," admits Bodine.

• Later that same year, leader Dale Jarrett loses his head — at least his helmet — after being bumped and forced out of a race at Tennessee's Bristol Raceway. Jarrett storms up to the edge of the track and waits for Bobby Hillin Jr. — the man he believes caused his crash — to come round again. As Hillin zooms by, Jarrett hoists up his helmet and heaves it at the car. "It's a shame idiots like that are out there," Jarrett says of Hillin.

• Michael Waltrip is mad as hell after being crowded by Lake Speed during the final laps of the 1995 Miller Genuine Draft 400 at Michigan International Speedway. As both drivers head into the pits, Waltrip cuts off Speed, hops out of his car and punches him twice. "He parked me like a highway patrolman," philosophizes Speed.

• Ted Musgrave nudges Ricky Rudd into a spinout during the 1995 Hanes 500 at Martinsville (Virginia) Speedway. Rudd's crew chief Bill Ingle decides a punch is just the ticket for Musgrave's driving infraction. Ingle cops a $250 fine for his delivery.

• There are two fights on the racing card at Dover (Delaware) Speedway in 1996. Post-race rumbles pit Kyle Petty against Michael Waltrip and Jimmy Spencer against Wally Dellenbach.

GOLFERS TEE OFF

• At a 1991 Senior PGA Tour event in Napa, California, golfers J.C. Snead and Dave Hill began clubbing each other before the shocked gallery gathered at the course practice range. Bug-eyed witnesses later linked the combatants' course language and actions to an errant drive by Snead. The mis-hit ball nearly clanged off a golf cart and nearly put a hole in one Joyce Hill. Her husband Dave was outraged by what he thought had been a deliberately aimed drive by Snead. So with club in hand, Hill charged across the range to engage Snead in a savage "sword fight" in a wild scene that resembled something straight out of a swashbuckler spectacular. Moments later, the senior swingers cast aside their clubs and began grappling hand-to-hand — a much more fair way of fighting for pro golfers. Snead and Hill were getting down and dirty by rolling on the grass. A posse of other players finally jumped in and pulled the punchers apart. Not so amazingly, neither golfer suffered injuries.

• Cyril Walker was arrested and carted off the golf course at the 1930 Los Angeles Open. His crime? Slow play! Walker's plodding style caused such an enormous traffic jam of players that officials urged him to hasten his game. When the past U.S. Open champion refused the plea for speed, he was disqualified. But he refused to leave the course.

Officials summoned police, who grabbed Walker by the elbows and rushed him off as he kicked and screamed in protest.

• NFL quarterbacks Casey Weldon and Trent Dilfer, teammates on the Tampa Bay Buccaneers, dropped their clubs and put up their dukes during an intensely competitive round at the Avila Country Club in 1996. Both combatants downplayed their brouhaha. But Tampa Bay's third signal caller, Craig Erickson, said Weldon and Dilfer did nothing wrong. "I love it," said Erickson. "We call it hate golf — you never, ever wish your opponent well."

> "MY THEORY ON FIGHTING IS DON'T FIGHT FAIR. SURPRISE THEM. GET THEM WHEN THEY'RE COMING OUT OF CHURCH."
>
> — *Houston Rockets guard Calvin Murphy, who at 5'9" was one of the smallest men to play pro basketball*

• Golfers needed police protection to compete in the 1914 Bamberger Trophy tournament in East Chester, New York. Prior to the event, the course caddies went on strike, seeking a quarter-a-round raise. Angry and out of work, the caddies resorted to stealing clubs from bags and balls from the fairways. They hurled insults at the golfers and clubbed anyone daring to carry their bags.

• Play had to be delayed at New Guinea's National Foursome championship when hostile tribes decided to settle their differences smack in the middle of the sixth fairway of the Port Moresby Golf Club in 1955. As the tribal tiff dragged on, police and club members grew impatient. They eventually put an end to the fairway fighting by arming themselves with golf clubs and driving off the combatants.

• From 1947 to 1973, the successful Oklahoma State golf program was run by the legendary Labron Harris, Sr. The former college wrestler and World War II martial arts instructor had little problem getting his golfers to pay attention — he'd knock them off their feet with a takedown move, then sit on them. Harris was tough, but fair. He introduced a "40-40" rule for students wanting to make the team. The qualifier rounds would be played unless the temperature dipped below 40 degrees and the wind was blowing greater than 40 miles per hour.

PEDAL PUNCHERS

Dutchman Michel Zanoli beat American Davis Phinney to the punch — literally — during the heated home stretch of the ninth stage of the 1992 Tour Du Pont bicycle race. The professional pedal-pushers were neck-and-neck as they sprinted furiously toward the finish line. Then the much-bigger biker from Holland hauled off and delivered a backhand blow that bloodied the nose and stained the uniform of the stunned U.S. cyclist at his side. The shameful punch smacked of poor sportsmanship and soon derailed any chance Zanoli had of winning the premier cycling event held on American soil. Tour Du Pont officials sprinted into action and unceremoniously ousted the 6'6", 200-pound puncher, effectively forcing Zanoli to pedal his talents elsewhere. Phinney, who had been rendered red-faced by the blow, never shifted gears with his game plan. The 5'9" cyclist vowed to push on, noting: "This ain't a boxing match."

ALL FOR GUN . . . AND GUN FOR BRAWL

• You could say South African soccer fans were extremely fired up after watching their beloved Umtata Bucks drubbed at home 6-0. Instead of aiming their anger at the pitiful players, angry fans targeted Bucks coach Walter da Silva as the cancer causing the poor play. Da Silva was at home when a mob of gun-toting Bucks backers came calling . . . for his immediate resignation. It was an offer the quaking coach could not refuse. Da Silva found himself over the barrel of a gun as he and his wife — and their two kids — packed their bags before being escorted to the airport and given a one-way ticket to Johannesburg. The armed mobbers were nice enough to give the stunned soccer coach a parting gift of $330.

• Terris McDuffie found out what it's like to pitch under the gun while playing winter league baseball in Cuba in the pre-Castro 1950s. The Negro League star was asked to pitch on two days' rest by manager Adolfo Luque. McDuffie balked at the assignment and informed his coach, "I'm going home." However, the locker-cleaning came to a sudden end when Luque waved a gun at his bug-eyed pitcher and asked, "Now, where are you going?" Swallowing hard, McDuffie answered: "I'm just getting ready to pitch. Give me the ball." He then took the mound and blew away the opposing batters with a nifty two-hit shutout.

• The turtle-paced play of a golfing foursome nearly triggered a deadly outburst at the Oxford Valley Golf Course in Levittown, Pennsylvania, in 1992. Lawrence Werner languished behind the slow-moving group for what seemed like an eternity. Then he blew his top and angrily confronted the quartet. Miffed by the irate intruder, one member of the foursome allegedly threatened Werner with his club. The reaction drove Werner to pull a gun. The gun-toting golfer was shoot out of luck when authorities caught up to him. As a matter of course, Werner was charged with reckless endangerment and disorderly conduct.

MANE EVENTS

With their horses straining neck-and-neck down the stretch of the 1933 Kentucky Derby, jockeys Herb Fisher and Don Meade started jockeying for prime position — by beating on each other! Meade was whipped into a fighting frenzy when Fisher attempted to slow his sprint for the finish line by pinning his pony up against the track's inside rail. Meade quickly tried to counter the crowding maneuver by letting go of his reins — and reaching for Fisher with the intent of shoving the jostling jockey off his horse! Fisher was able to fend off Meade by whacking him with his crop. Despite such mid-race meddling, Meade managed to win the raucous Run for the Roses by a nose. The shameful tactics trotted out by both rough riders left the hallowed horse race with a black eye and a new nickname — The Dirty Derby. Racing officials weren't horsing around when they slapped Fisher and Meade with 30-day suspensions. Neither jockey mounted a challenge.

UPI/Corbis-Bettmann

H. W. FISHER GIVES NEW MEANING TO "JOCKEYING FOR POSITION."

• Olympic pentathlete Hans-Jurgen Todt drew a beautiful, but stubborn horse named Ranchero to ride during the 1968 Summer Games in Mexico City. The West German quickly became infuriated when his mount refused to jump over three separate obstacles along the course. After completing his horrible round, the angry Todt attacked the horse with his fists! Teammates had to rein in the crazed rider.

• Female jockey Vicky Aragon went a bit too heavy on the crop in 1986 leading to a pair of suspensions for whipping fellow riders — in the middle of two different races! First, Aragon and Marty Wentz were fined and suspended for beating each other with their whips. A few weeks later, Aragon was back in the saddle, but hadn't learned her lesson. During a race, she spared her horse and began whacking jockey Victor Mercado on the head for no apparent reason. Officials attempted to whip Aragon into shape by handing her a three-week suspension.

NASTIE BEHAVIOR

During his match with Deon Joubert at the 1982 Dutch Open, ill-tempered tennis star Ilie Nastase served up a perfect example of his legendary tantrum-tossing antics. "Nastie" went nuts when a linesman's ruling on a close call didn't go his way. Nastase completely lost his cool and charged into the stands to scoop up a full tray of ice cream cones from the trembling hands of a terrified vendor. Then, the Romanian flipped out even more by flinging the ice cream cones at stunned members of the crowd. Outraged Ilie then dished out what he believed to be just desserts for the linesman who triggered his tirade. In plain view of the shocked crowd and match officials, Nastase cornered the courtside official and smeared ice cream all over him. Dutch Open officials were amazingly good-humored over Ilie's nasty outburst. The ice cream man went unpunished and was allowed to play on!

NASTASE NEVER PLACED SECOND IN GAMESMANSHIP.

UPI/Corbis-Bettmann

BLOOD IS THICKER . . .

Sports brawls sunk to a new low in 1956 when Russian and Hungarian water polo players used their feet, hands, elbows and knees to make waves — and contact with each other — during a wild and woolly match in Melbourne, Australia. The athletes learned

THIS WATER POLO MATCH MUST HAVE FEATURED MALLETS.

UPI/Corbis-Bettmann

firsthand that blood is indeed thicker than water as they whacked away at each other during the frenzied final minutes of the match won by Hungary, 4-0. Ervin Zador, captain of the victorious squad, needed medical attention to close a nasty cut opened near his right eye by a Russian player. The rough play of the Russians churned up the crowd and triggered a deafening chorus of boos throughout the December 8 debacle which nearly ended in a poolside riot.

> ## "I'M A BLUE COLLAR WORKER — I DON'T PUNCH IN, I PUNCH OUT."
>
> — *New York Knicks forward Maurice Lucas*

INDEX

INDEX

INDEX

INDEX

INDEX

INDEX